CHRIST THE APOSTLE

Ministry Model For The Ages

Apostle Stephen A. Garner

ISBN # 978-1719339278
Printed in the United States of America

TABLE OF CONTENTS

Introduction - Page 1

Chapter 1 – Page 5
CHRIST THE BUILDER OF THE CHURCH

Chapter 2 – Page 10
CHRIST THE DELIVER OF THE DEMONIZED

Chapter 3 – Page 15
CHRIST THE HEALER OF SICKNESS & DISEASE

Chapter 4 – Page 21
CHRIST THE AMBASSADOR OF THE KINGDOM

Chapter 5 – Page 28
CHRIST THE SENDER OF MINISTRY GIFTS

Chapter 6 – Page 39
CHRIST THE BLUEPRINT FOR INTERCESSION

Chapter 7 – Page 47
CHRIST THE TEACHER AND DISPENSER
OF DOCTRINE

Chapter 8 – Page 53
THE PREACHING MINISTRY OF CHRIST

Chapter 9 – Page 57
CHRIST THE ULTIMATE TEAM BUILDER

INTRODUCTION

Hebrews 3:1 (KJV)
Wherefore, holy brethren, partakers of the heavenly calling, consider the Apostle and High Priest of our profession, Christ Jesus;

The ministry of Christ is the ultimate pattern. No other model in my estimation is worthy of duplicating other than His. Everything about His ministry revealed eternity's agenda for the furtherance of His Kingdom. I'm convinced that learning of Him and purposing to impose His agenda above all else will yield a harvest of great proportion.

Hebrews 3:1 gives perspective of His ministry that many perhaps haven't looked at. Christ here is declared to be the apostle and high priest of our profession. Many see Christ as the Son of God, Redeemer, Lord, Savior, Healer, etc., but not as our apostle. The words apostle and consider unlocks this verse to a truth I deem necessary for effective ministry, that will influence the times and seasons of generations to come.

The word Consider means to think about and be drawn towards, to regard as having a specific quality, to take into account when making a judgment or assessment.

We are to be drawn towards Christ and begin to think of Him as an apostle. This paradigm of thought will create the proper mental templates for studying the ministry of an apostle and the works ascribed to this office.

A working definition of the word apostle is necessary as well. The word apostle isn't a spiritual term in its origin. The ancient Greeks when sending envoys to nations coming under their rule would deploy their apostles to lead them. Their job was to assure the arrival of the vested interest of Greeks ruling power in the territory they were sent to. In brief the word apostle means one sent as the representative of another.

Apostle is a transliterated word, one that is taken directly from another language with little change. Apostle is taken from the Greek word apostolos. This word literally means "one sent forth." Apo literally means "from" and stolos comes from stello, which means "I send." Within the New Testament and in other classical Greek literature, apostolos has the simple meaning of "one sent as a representative of another," the representative deriving his authority and power from the one sending him. This simple definition is the root meaning of apostle. – Roger Sapp

Christ was God's sent one, He was sent by God as a legal representation of heaven. He was tasked with establishing the Kingdom of God on the earth. He was also mandate to colonize territories and convert them into spiritual outpost in order to make the lands influenced by Him eventually be conduits for heaven to have expression on the earth. His mission was to bring the vested interest of eternity, the government of God and the fullness of His Kingdom into the earth. Christ would accomplish this in part by preaching, teaching and demonstrating the Kingdom of God and executing the government of the Kingdom everywhere He went.

His apostolic ministry powerfully impacted the people of the lands within the grid He was sent. Those who were inundated with darkness saw great light. Widows had their sons raised from the dead. Blind eyes were open, dumb tongues loosed and death ears were unstopped.

The Kingdom of God was in full operation and advancing its cause because of the One sent by God. Christ repentance and declared the ushering in of a new time. Eternity was imposing itself upon the earth with full force. Nothing could stop it.

Prophecy after prophecy was being fulfilled and history was being written and the narrative of humanity was suddenly experiencing transformation. Standards congruent with holiness and righteousness were exacted in the earth. Entire families were elevated from the dunghills of life. A true Change Agent had come.

Christ would eventually pay the ultimate price for our redemption. However the work He began as an apostle was ordained to continue from generation to generation. He commissioned others to do as He Himself had done. Apostles today are to follow the same pattern. That is to proclaim the Kingdom of God and all its vast intricacies. They are also tasked with demonstrating it and building trans-generationally as Christ did.

As you read this book my prayer is for the eyes of your understanding to be enlightened. I pray that you will develop a working understanding of Christ apostolic ministry and its importance in the Church today. May grace be imparted to function seamlessly with Him and His apostolic ministry.

CHAPTER 1

CHRIST THE BUILDER OF HIS CHURCH

Matthew 16:18-19 KJV
And I say also unto thee, That thou art Peter, and upon this rock I will build my church; and the gates of hell shall not prevail against it. 19 And I will give unto thee the keys of the kingdom of heaven: and whatsoever thou shalt bind on earth shall be bound in heaven: and whatsoever thou shalt loose on earth shall be loosed in heaven.

Several things are happening in this passage we need to look at so we can develop perhaps a deeper appreciation and understanding for Christ and His apostleship. I want to provide these occurrences as points first and then expound just a bit more afterwards.

1) Identity is established to the one who has a revelation of who Christ is. Apostles help bring clarity to those who share in the responsibility of building with them. Christ model for apostolic ministry is to bring clarity to His followers and co-laborers in the place of identity.
2) Christ is doing the building and He will supply the assurance and the grace required for those who partner

with Him to build apostolically. Power will emerge. Rise above the frustrations that arise against us as we partner with Him.

3) Christ proclaims victory before any battle or warfare is initiated. He declares the end of a thing before the beginning. He's the chief architecture.

4) Christ provides a working knowledge of what is and what's to come by bringing us into the knowledge of His master plan for the Church. This insight empowers us to make a wise investment with our lives as those He will send to represent Him.

5) Keys are given to establish His commands. These keys also empower us to exercise the authority given unto to us in both the natural and spiritual realms.

The building dimension of the apostle's ministry is one of necessity. Apostles are burdened with constructing ministry according to the design and pattern of eternity. Christ as the apostle of our profession has laid the groundwork for the design and building of His Church. His bold declaration according to Matthew 16:18-19 secures His Church of not succumbing the powers of hell, but rather assures us of victory over the powers of darkness because He is taking personal responsibility to construct us in such a way that we are hell proofed.

From its inception through its maturity, Christ was deeply involved and powerfully impacting the membership of His Church. This is to be viewed in the context of people. Jesus as our apostle is concerned about the lives of the believers being built in accordance to our creators mandate. The overall effectiveness of any local church will be in direct proportion to the proper constructing of its membership. While many are majoring on the aesthetics of their ministry or the numbers of their organization, Christ is concerned about the constructing and development of His people.

He was committed to empowering the membership by imparting authority and ability necessary to influence both the natural and spirit realm. There are so many believers who are clueless about the spiritual things. They lack understanding and articulation concerning the things of the spirit. Christ apostolic ministry is geared towards building people who are effective in both natural and spiritual things.

There are myriads of believers all around the globe who have succumb to the powers of darkness. The strongholds over their societies working with the principalities for many have produced insurmountable odds. Many are forced to simply operate in the shadows of their respective regions. They are limited to perhaps a cultural expression of the Church and live under the dictates of darkness. The laws and policies that shape their culture determine the level of their worship and commitment to Christ.

The Lord challenged the culture of His day and didn't allow the policies of the land or the laws to dictate how He served our Father. He was sent by God to inaugurate the Kingdom of God. The Church was the conduit He chose to do so. Therefore He had to build it in such a way as to not be subject to the powers of the age. As a result wherever His Church gathers, apostles are needed to reinforce the truths established by Christ, the apostle of our profession, in order to secure, in our day, the victory He established for the ages.

Foundation is extremely important when it comes to building. The doctrinal foundation of the Church will determine how we are configured and how we comply with Christ. The structural integrity of and building is based upon the depth and design of its foundation. Christ has laid a foundation that is consistent with eternity. Apostolic ministries that will have eternal manifestations and build works that endure through the ages will have a strong emphasis on foundation.

Apostles today who have partnered with Christ and His apostolic ministry will build by Gods blueprint and design for His Church. He has set them in the Church first to serve as a model. They realize their credibility is directly connected to their adherence to God's patterns.

They embrace Christ as their model and purpose to build with Him. They share His burden to assure that the Church declares Gods wisdom for the ages and serves as the pillar and ground of truth.

CHAPTER 2

CHRIST THE DELIVERER OF THE DEMONIZED

Mark 1:39 KJV

And he preached in their synagogues throughout all Galilee, and cast out devils.

The ministry of deliverance is one of primary ways Christ manifested His Kingdom and demonstrated power over demons inside of the people to whom He was sent. The advancement of the Kingdom mandates the preaching of deliverance. Jesus preached deliverance to the captives and then demonstrated power over their captors. (demons)

His deliverance ministry was public and highly visible. He made no apologies for it and challenged the powers of darkness in every territory He was sent. One of the visible signs of an apostle's ministry is that of deliverance. Those joined to them will not only receive deliverance, but receive training to minister deliverance as well.

Notice how in the referenced verse Jesus preached and then cast out demons. Apostles who pattern themselves after Christ will also demonstrate power over demonic forces. Christ will work with them and assure they experience victorious works as they partner with Him to advance His Kingdom.

Matthew 8:16 KJV
When the even was come, they brought unto him many that were possessed with devils: and he cast out the spirits with his word, and healed all that were sick:

The doctrine of an apostle is extremely vital in making accurate inroads into foreign regions. This is also true when it comes deprogramming the lifestyles and mindsets of people. The apostle's doctrine is extremely critical to the deliverance of those to whom they are sent. Jesus cast out the spirits operating in people who were brought to Him with His words. There's an authority God puts within apostles to challenge demonic powers.

Many will shy away from the ministry of deliverance because of fear of being marginalized or excluded from certain circuits of ministry. The fear of being labeled as a proponent of heretical teaching is also an issue. While others won't give themselves to the labor this ministry mandates, God will put an abundance of grace on those He sends to cast out devils. They will also possess the boldness necessary to promote this most vital part of the apostolic ministry.

Matthew 4:15-16 KJV

The land of Zabulon, and the land of Nephthalim, by the way of the sea, beyond Jordan, Galilee of the Gentiles; 16 The people which sat in darkness saw great light; and to them which sat in the region and shadow of death light is sprung up.

Christ had a circuit He preached on. Within that circuit He demonstrated the ministry of deliverance. Those who sat in darkness saw great light and those appointed to death encountered life. The apostle's ministry will often include a circuit they're sent by God to impact. The first 10 years of my ministry I frequented the continent of Africa. Tremendous breakthrough and manifestations of the supernatural were made manifest. Casting out demons was a constant part of my assignment. The Lord was working with me and confirming His word.

Matthew 12:28 KJV

But if I cast out devils by the Spirit of God, then the kingdom of God is come unto you.

Christ had one focus and that was the advancement of the Kingdom of God. All of His works would culminate in the Kingdom manifesting in the earth, not in the context of the terra firma only, but within the people He was sent to. Delivering them from the demons working in them was paramount to this becoming a reality.

Failure to do so would restrict them from manifesting the Kingdom of God. Christ knew that people would accept His message, but be rendered ineffective in advancing His Kingdom if demonic spirits aren't driven out. Righteousness, peace and joy are all attributes of the Kingdom of God and all of hells host are working to prevent these attributes from manifest through people. Christ as our apostle made casting out demons a pivotal part of His ministry.

Ephesians 5:11 KJV
And have no fellowship with the unfruitful works of darkness, but rather reprove them.

Demons are creatures of darkness. They thrive in darkness and obscurity. They hate light. Jesus declares He is the Light of world and in Him there's no darkness at all. As our pattern apostle, Christ was disengaged from the powers of darkness. He was both the message and messenger of light. He preached freedom, redemption and breakthrough. He also reproved the works of darkness. Reprove means to rebuke. A vital part of an apostle's ministry is to proclaim light, the glorious light of the Gospel of Christ. The powers of darkness hate this because the light makes manifest their evil works against humanity.

A critical part to destroying the yokes of darkness that are working against the multitudes is exposing them through preaching. Demons hate the message of deliverance and the messengers as well. They know their unfruitful works will be rendered ineffective and their schemes to hold people captive will be rooted out. Christ was on a mission when He walked this planet to liberate the bound as an apostle. This mandate hasn't changed.

Mark 16:17 implies that casting out demons is a part of the Great Commission. I'm convinced that many will not be able to come into the fullness of their destiny without receiving deliverance. Therefore God must have those whom He can send to preach and demonstrate the ministry of deliverance.

Today's apostles who pattern their ministry after Christ will have a visible deliverance ministry where demons are cast out. They understand the advancement of the Kingdom of God mandates this ministry cultivated in them. They also give themselves to training and developing others to preach deliverance and cast out demons. This will be a seal of their apostleship in those who are joined to them.

CHAPTER 3

CHRIST THE HEALER OF SICKNESS & DISEASE

God's first reference to His people after their deliverance from Egyptian captivity according to Exodus 15:26 was that He was their healer. He hasn't changed His orientation. Christ as an apostle is therefore obligated to demonstrate the power of God in the area of healing. I believe that every apostle should have a burden for healing. It's difficult to raise up people who are responsible for advancing the Kingdom of God if they are sick and infirmed.

Healing and divine health are the will of God. 3 John 2 KJV Beloved, I wish above all things that thou mayest prosper and be in health even as thy soul prospereth. Adam and Eve were perfect and void of any sickness. They prospered and enjoyed the best of life. Unfortunately the fall of Adam and Eve to sin opened humanity up to a myriad of issues. The kingdom of darkness deployed sickness and disease and the whole of the human race has been affected. Christ apostolic mission includes healing and the redemption of our bodies. Many have become immobilized and taken out prematurely because of sickness or disease. I believe our local assemblies and the Global Church should thrive in the area of healing. Let's look in brief at Christ healing mission.

Acts 10:38 KJV
How God anointed Jesus of Nazareth with the Holy
Ghost and with power: who went about doing good, and
healing all that were oppressed of the devil; for God was
with him.

Sickness is a part of Satan's evil scheme to oppress the
whole of humanity. God anointed Christ as a sent one to
heal those oppressed of the devil. The word oppressed
means to have dominion exercised over you or against
you. God designed us with dominion in mind. Christ
apostleship was that of restoration and healing which is
a necessary part of the restoration process. Christ gave
Himself to the ministry of healing. He realized that if
people were to be empowered to advance His Kingdom
He needed to heal them.

Mark 1:32-34 KJV
And at even, when the sun did set, they brought unto
him all that were diseased, and them that were
possessed with devils. 33 And all the city was gathered
together at the door. 34 And he healed many that were
sick of divers diseases, and cast out many devils; and
suffered not the devils to speak, because they knew him.

Healing was central to Christ apostolic ministry because
it's directly connected to salvation and the establishing
of the New Covenant. Isaiah prophesies that part of
Christ redemptive work on the cross was for our

healing but His literal ministry as a sent one mandated He heal the sick. Healing is also connected to the realm of signs and wonders. Jesus declares except you see signs and wonders you won't believe. Therefore in order to liberate many from unbelief healing must be demonstrated.

Over the last 15 years of ministry from 2003 until 2018 I've learned that there are two prevailing issues in the whole of humanity, demons and sickness. Christ apostolic ministry dealt with roots in the lives of those whom He was sent to. Sickness and infirmity doesn't respect any demographic of people. It crosses all socio economic boundaries. It doesn't respect any pedigree or category of people. From environmental issues and genetic disorder as a result of sin, sickness and disease has interwoven themselves into the whole of humanity.

Jesus was on a mission as heavens ambassador to demonstrate power over sickness and disease. His apostleship wasn't governed by a bunch of intellectual jargon that tickled the ears of the multitudes, but one of power to liberate them from physical and mental ailments that had debilitated their health. He preached the Kingdom of God and then flowed in power to heal the sick and make the diseased whole.

Mark 1:32-34 gives a synopsis of His apostleship in action as a healer. Multitudes of demonized and diseased people were brought to Him. An entire city came to partake of the apostolic grace on Him and receive deliverance from their demons and have their bodies and minds restored from the damning effects of their infirmities.

Matthew 12:22 KJV

Then was brought unto him one possessed with a devil, blind, and dumb: and he healed him, insomuch that the blind and dumb both spake and saw.

Matthew 9:32-33 KJV

32 As they went out, behold, they brought to him a dumb man possessed with a devil. 33 And when the devil was cast out, the dumb spake: and the multitudes marvelled, saying, It was never so seen in Israel.

Luke 8:1-3 KJV

And it came to pass afterward, that he went throughout every city and village, preaching and shewing the glad tidings of the kingdom of God: and the twelve were with him, 2 And certain women, which had been healed of evil spirits and infirmities, Mary called Magdalene, out of whom went seven devils, 3 And Joanna the wife of Chuza Herod's steward, and Susanna, and many others, which ministered unto him of their substance.

Luke 13:10-13 KJV
And he was teaching in one of the synagogues on the sabbath. 11 And, behold, there was a woman which had a spirit of infirmity eighteen years, and was bowed together, and could in no wise lift up herself. 12 And when Jesus saw her, he called her to him, and said unto her, Woman, thou art loosed from thine infirmity. 13 And he laid his hands on her: and immediately she was made straight, and glorified God.

There are several references where Jesus was moving in a healing anointing and demons were cast out then healing would manifest. Multitudes are held captive by hell and incapacitated in their walk for Christ because of physical ailments. They are needed to advance the Kingdom of God and Christ is releasing an army of sent ones to liberate them from the holds of darkness placed upon them.

Matthew 14:14 KJV
And Jesus went forth, and saw a great multitude, and was moved with compassion toward them, and he healed their sick.

Compassion for the welfare of the masses was a burden Christ carried. He demonstrated this compassion by healing them of their sickness. Apostles will be dispensers of tremendous amounts of compassion for the masses. They'll utilize their resources to gather them for times of empowerment. They'll also be mobile and go to distant lands and dark places around the globe demonstrating the power of God over sickness. Healing, signs and wonders help to validate and substantiate those called to apostolic ministry.

Today's apostles will give themselves to develop in the area of healing. They will teach on this subject often and build within their immediate sphere an environment full of faith for the supernatural. Notable signs concerning healing will be manifested through them. There will also be an emphasis placed on healing teams. They'll be deployed to go to remote places to demonstrate this ministry.

CHAPTER 4

CHRIST THE AMBASSADOR OF THE KINGDOM

Matthew 4:17-20

From that time Jesus began to preach, and to say, Repent: for the kingdom of heaven is at hand. 18 And Jesus, walking by the sea of Galilee, saw two brethren, Simon called Peter, and Andrew his brother, casting a net into the sea: for they were fishers. 19And he saith unto them, Follow me, and I will make you fishers of men. 20 And they straightway left their nets, and followed him.

The message of the Kingdom was the central theme of Christ apostolic ministry. His coming was rooted in the restoration of all things. In order for restoration to fully manifest the Kingdom of God had to be established in the earth. Jesus was sent by God to inaugurate the Kingdom on the earth. Jesus began preaching repent for the Kingdom of Heaven is at hand. Repentance is necessary for the Kingdom of Heaven, an invisible kingdom to be made manifest. Repent literally means to change the way you think. Christ apostolic mandate was comprised of a message designed to help those to whom He was sent to change the way they think.

2 Corinthians 10:3-5 KJV

For though we walk in the flesh, we do not war after the flesh: 4 (For the weapons of our warfare are not carnal, but mighty through God to the pulling down of strong holds;) 5 Casting down imaginations, and every high thing that exalteth itself against the knowledge of God, and bringing into captivity every thought to the obedience of Christ;

Apostolic ministry isn't geared towards utilizing carnal or fleshly means to advance the purposes of God, but rather that, which is of Gods Spirit. The weapons deployed are wrought in God and they are mighty indeed. The word warfare opens the text up and gives credence to the work of an apostle. It comes from the Greek word *strateia* where the word strategy comes from and it means a military service, the apostolic career as one of hardship and danger. Christ literally waged a military campaign. His mission for advancing the Kingdom of God on the earth initiated a war against the kingdom of darkness. Apostles will draw scrutiny and resistance inspired by demonic forces as they align with Christ to advance His campaign.

Christ systematically challenged outdated mindsets within the people of His apostolic sphere. He challenged their carnal inclinations and addressed their flawed paradigms of thinking concerning the things of God. The religious leaders of that day and the system of worship they became diehards for what was being challenged by the government of God. There was a divine shift, God was moving away from what was deeply engrained in the psyche of Israel, and their prophets foretold this move, yet they were blinded to it. They were looking for the restoration of an earthly physical kingdom. However Christ was sent to pioneer a spiritual Kingdom, one of power and authority. This Kingdom could only be accessed through faith in Christ and a born again experience.

His message stirred up anger and great indignation. The ministry of an apostle at times will provoke those who are resistant to change and heavens agenda to manifest hostilities. Warfare is necessary at times in order to make inroads into dark places territorially or within the minds of people in order to liberate them from erroneous ways of thinking.

God's Kingdom came with power and Christ was leading the charge. A new era was initiated and the narrative of the masses was being changed before their eyes. Apostles believe in and advocate for the power of God to manifest. They will challenge corruption, false doctrine, error, heretical works and anything that promotes falsehood and dishonor. They'll often be viewed as being the very thing they confront. They will display tremendous passion for the advancement of the

Kingdom. They will preach and teach the Kingdom of God with authority.

Acts 1:3 KJV
To whom also he shewed himself alive after his passion by many infallible proofs, being seen of them forty days, and speaking of the things pertaining to the kingdom of God:

Apostles today must have a working knowledge of the Kingdom of God. The capacity of an apostle and apostolic people to articulate and demonstrate the Kingdom is imperative to forming invasions that will yield people who value the Kingdom of God. After the Lord's resurrection from the dead He demonstrates His passion for the Kingdom by many infallible proofs and continues proclaiming the Kingdom of God.

Today's apostles will continue in declaring the Kingdom of God. The ministries joined to them and the works they promote will undeniably be built to propagate the advancement of God's Kingdom. They will give themselves to develop systematic teachings on the Kingdom of God. They will often base their discipleship curriculum on the Kingdom of God and have the value system of the King intricately interwoven into all they aspire to do. The fruit will be the emergence of a victorious people who are trained and developed in doctrine and in deeds who know how to manifest the Kingdom of God.

What is the Kingdom of God comprised of?
Romans 14:17-18 KJV
For the kingdom of God is not meat and drink; but righteousness, and peace, and joy in the Holy Ghost. 18 For he that in these things serveth Christ is acceptable to God, and approved of men.

How do I gain access to the Kingdom of God?

John 3:3-5 KJV
Jesus answered and said unto him, Verily, verily, I say unto thee, Except a man be born again, he cannot see the kingdom of God. 4 Nicodemus saith unto him, How can a man be born when he is old? can he enter the second time into his mother's womb, and be born? 5 Jesus answered, Verily, verily, I say unto thee, Except a man be born of water and of the Spirit, he cannot enter into the kingdom of God.

Where is the Kingdom of God?

Luke 17:20-21 KJV
And when he was demanded of the Pharisees, when the kingdom of God should come, he answered them and said, The kingdom of God cometh not with observation: 21 Neither shall they say, Lo here! or, lo there! for,

behold, the kingdom of God is within you.

Who is disqualified for Kingdom of God?

1 Corinthians 6:9-11 KJV
Know ye not that the unrighteous shall not inherit the kingdom of God? Be not deceived: neither fornicators, nor idolaters, nor adulterers, nor effeminate, nor abusers of themselves with mankind, 10 Nor thieves, nor covetous, nor drunkards, nor revilers, nor extortioners, shall inherit the kingdom of God. 11 And such were some of you: but ye are washed, but ye are sanctified, but ye are justified in the name of the Lord Jesus, and by the Spirit of our God.

What does the Kingdom of God do?

Daniel 2:44 KJV
And in the days of these kings shall the God of heaven set up a kingdom, which shall never be destroyed: and the kingdom shall not be left to other people, but it shall break in pieces and consume all these kingdoms, and it shall stand for ever.

How can we release the Kingdom?

Luke 11:2 KJV
And he said unto them, When ye pray, say, Our Father which art in heaven, Hallowed be thy name. Thy

kingdom come. Thy will be done, as in heaven, so in earth.

What advantage is gained by seeking the Kingdom of God?

Luke 12:29-32 KJV
And seek not ye what ye shall eat, or what ye shall drink, neither be ye of doubtful mind.30 For all these things do the nations of the world seek after: and your Father knoweth that ye have need of these things. 31 But rather seek ye the kingdom of God; and all these things shall be added unto you.

CHAPTER 5

CHRIST THE SENDER OF MINISTRY GIFTS

John 20:21-23 KJV

Then said Jesus to them again, Peace be unto you: as my Father hath sent me, even so send I you. 22 And when he had said this, he breathed on them, and saith unto them, Receive ye the Holy Ghost: 23 Whosoever sins ye remit, they are remitted unto them; and whosoever sins ye retain, they are retained.

The sending dimension of Christ apostolic ministry is extremely vital to the overall advancement of his ministry throughout the ages. Individuals must be raised, equipped and empowered to do what He Himself has done. He is committed to this and has promised to work with us and confirm His word with signs following according to Mark 16:20. Apostolic oversight is something Christ has validated and I believe is a pattern that should be embraced today.

Every generation needs to have an accurate representation of Christ in order to operate effectively and be in compliance with Him. Apostles in particular are tasked with the mission of representing Christ. They are tasked with upholding truths, promoting doctrine, advocating righteousness and adhering to the counsel of heaven, just to name a few.

John 17:17-18 KJV

Sanctify them through thy truth: thy word is truth. 18 As thou hast sent me into the world, even so have I also sent them into the world.

Jesus is interceding on behalf of those He would send. He's asking the Father to sanctify us through His truth because He was sending us into the world as He was sent. The hostilities, grace, capacity, strength, wisdom, inner resolve, sanctification and all Christ utilized are necessary for those He sends as well. Therefore a continual renewal of our dependency on Him is important for us to abide steadfast in representing Him. A thorough acquaintance of His apostolic sphere and mantle is a necessity.

Matthew 10:1 KJV

And when he had called unto him his twelve disciples, he gave them power against unclean spirits, to cast them out, and to heal all manner of sickness and all manner of disease.

Matthew 10:5-8 KJV

These twelve Jesus sent forth, and commanded them, saying, Go not into the way of the Gentiles, and into any city of the Samaritans enter ye not: 6 But go rather to the lost sheep of the house of Israel. 7 And as ye go, preach, saying, The kingdom of heaven is at hand. 8 Heal the sick, cleanse the lepers, raise the dead, cast out devils: freely ye have received, freely give.

These verses give us insight into what Jesus sent those charged with representing Him to do. Remember that the one who is sent derives their authority and power to function from the one who sends them. He first gave them power, which gives the connotation of ability. This power was twofold. It was necessary to cast out demonic spirits and for healing the sick. In my travels and ministry tenure I've witnessed two things consistent with all people, demons and sickness. There is no ethnic group exempt. Demonized people and those who are sick will prove difficult to develop when it comes to advancing the Kingdom of God. Demons will restrict people from cultivating fruit and sickness will restrict them from being available and mobile.

Christ sends them forth to preach the Kingdom and demonstrate its supremacy over the powers of darkness. Those sent by Christ according to the text are given simple instructions that are almost inconceivable when you think of the vast needs in any given society. However there's wisdom in the verses we need to look at. When a person hears the message of the Kingdom they become recipients of Good News. They'll be exposed to forgiveness, redemption and right standing with God. Their lives will be exposed to the resources of the King of the Kingdom. He will position them to reign in life and manifest His Kingdom as well.

Luke 11:49 KJV
Therefore also said the wisdom of God, I will send them prophets and apostles, and some of them they shall slay and persecute:

Apostles and prophets are sent by the wisdom of God. They are tasked with manifesting the wisdom of God in the territories they are sent. The wisdom of God is necessary to build and develop people properly. Every people group, nation or territory is not the same. The needs will vary and the wisdom of God is required to minister the plans of eternity sanctioned. 1 Corinthians 3:10 implies that apostles are wise master builders, which speaks of a chief constructor or architect. Apostles know how to interpret heavens blueprints and convert those blueprints by the wisdom of God and develop His people. Failure to build by the blueprints of heaven will often time result in a lack of presence and power. God isn't obligated to dwell in a system or structure that's not built according to His design and pattern.

Men have sought to build by their own wisdom and blueprints. They construct elaborate facilities, garner tremendous wealth and have platforms of high visibility. These things are grand and necessary, but they don't qualify that work to be a conduit for eternal things inspired by God to manifest in the earth. Religion and dead works that lack in glory, power, revelation, impartation, presence and breakthrough often emerge as a result. The issue is the wisdom of God isn't there because the wisdom of man has been sought above it.

Proverbs 9:1-3 KJV
Wisdom hath builded her house, she hath hewn out her seven pillars:
2 She hath killed her beasts; she hath mingled her wine; she hath also furnished her table. 3 She hath sent forth her maidens: she crieth upon the highest places of the city,

Here there are several things listed that will manifest as the wisdom of God is deployed. Wisdom carries capacity to build. Wisdom hewns out here 7 pillars, which is a picture of bringing completion and carving out mature works. Wisdom kills her beast, which is a picture of demonic spirits. Wisdom mingles her wine, which references the Spirit of God. Wisdom helps to engage the things of the Spirit properly. Wisdom furnishes her table. There is a realm of legislation and advocacy every mandate of heaven requires. Gathering at a table or place to enact policies are necessary. Wisdom empowers those sent by God to do so. Wisdom sends forth her maidens, which is a picture of a team or helps ministry. Every apostle needs a team and wisdom will supply this most vital resource. Wisdom cries from the highest places of the city. Satan hates true apostles and will do whatever he can to limit their visibility and influence. Wisdom will promote and help elevate the presence of apostles in their cities and ministry grids.

Those Whom God Sent

Apostolic people are extremely important when it comes to the implementation of initiatives consistent with heaven. These believers are highly prophetic and articulate. They have within them a sensitivity to the Spirit of God and the spirit world. They have an inner resolve to breakthrough and obey God at all cost. They have purposed to execute Gods will and embraced His charged as the substance that will sustain them. The finish is their target and an unwavering faith committed to advancing God's Kingdom is their ultimate drive.

Genesis 45:7 KJV
And God sent me before you to preserve you a posterity in the earth, and to save your lives by a great deliverance.

Joseph is an apostolic type. He was sent by God into Egypt and his assignment was not short of warfare. Even though Joseph was sold into slavery by his siblings, he was promoted because the hand of God was upon his life. Wrongfully accused of improprieties that could have cost him his life, but he prevails by the grace of God. His warfare was grueling to say the least. After 12 years of incarceration his life changes in an instant.

The day came when Pharaoh, Joseph's oppressor, summonsed and elevated him to fulfill his destiny. Those whom God sends must purpose to live free from bitterness and live aligned with the ministry of reconciliation. The wisdom of God in Joseph both preserved and saved a vast majority of humanity within his territorial grid. There is a preserving and saving dimension to the Joseph type of apostolic believers. They will thrive in business and market place environments.

Exodus 3:10 KJV
Come now therefore, and I will send thee unto Pharaoh, that thou mayest bring forth my people the children of Israel out of Egypt.

Moses is an apostolic type. He was sent by God to deal with the satanic forces working through the Pharaoh of his day who was bent on keeping Israel in captivity. Moses is a clear expression of the delivering dimension of the apostolic. He was sent with a miracle mantle that enacted successive waves of Gods judgment against the oppressive forces of darkness operating against the Lords inheritance.

Moses was a man of fasting, prayer and encounter. His ministry was based on intimacy and the power of God. His apostolic ministry was one that preserved and delivered as Joseph's, but through signs and wonders. Moses type apostolic believers have a tangible hunger for the power of God and the realm of miracles will be a signet of their works.

Nehemiah 2:6 KJV
And the king said unto me, (the queen also sitting by him,) For how long shall thy journey be? and when wilt thou return? So it pleased the king to send me; and I set him a time.

Nehemiah is an apostolic type. His commission to go and build came by way of a burden he received by way of a report concerning the welfare of his people (Nehemiah 1:1-4). His allegiance to king Artaxerxes as his cupbearer placed him in both a favorable and precarious situation simultaneously. He's privileged to stand in the presence of the king, but his responsibility daily could lead to his personal demise. After a time of fasting and prayer Nehemiah goes and articulates his burden to Artaxerxes.

The king sends Nehemiah to restore the walls that was in ruin and disrepair. Nehemiah also goes with the favor of the king. He has letters given to him from Artaxerxes to access all of his resources. Those who are sent by God will have the assurance of heavens resources. Favor will be upon them and the territories they're sent to will open up to them. God will endow them with wisdom to subdue opposing forces. They will bring restoration and resurrect hope among the people. Families will experience the healing power of God and alignment with heavens agenda will prevail. Nehemiah type apostolic believers are graced to bring comfort and restoration.

Isaiah 6:8 KJV
Also I heard the voice of the Lord, saying, Whom shall I send, and who will go for us? Then said I, Here am I; send me.

Isaiah is an apostolic type. His mandate was to declare God's displeasure with Israel because of their violations of God's. Isaiah was burdened with declaring the future and the coming of the Messiah. His messages were both confrontational and out of the box.

Isaiah has an encounter with the angelic realm and something of divine magnitude is loosed in his life. The Godhead needed one they could send to speak on their behalf. Isaiah avails himself and heaven has an ambassador active to bring forth the biddings of eternity. Isaiah type apostolic believers are highly prophetic. They have seized the pulse of heaven and have a sense of urgency working in them to move within the time frame of God. They help the Church come out of obscurity, greed, idolatry and confusion.

John 1:6-7 KJV

There was a man sent from God, whose name was John. 7 The same came for a witness, to bear witness of the Light, that all men through him might believe.

John is an apostolic type. He was dubbed by Christ as being the greatest of all prophets according to Luke 7:28. John was a forerunner for Christ. There are apostolic voices commissioned to prepare cities, regions, nations and territories for Christ. This is a formidable work. These types of apostles and apostolic people are better than any of the other types, but bear a responsibility of greater magnitude in my estimation.

John announced the expiration of one season and announced the inauguration of a new one. He was a voice and provided context and content for that which had come as prophesied in the scriptures. John's apostolic model as a sent one was adherent to the fulfillment of divine time lines. There is a demographic of sent ones set to fulfill divine time lines in order to keep the Body of Christ compliant with heavenly mandates. They give constant witness to the current dealings of the Light of The World (Christ) in order to keep the Church on the cutting edge. Their ministries are revelatory and outside the order of man. They will have a supernatural draw. People from all walks of life will be drawn to them, especially prophetic people burdened with the urgency of the future.

CHAPTER 6

CHRIST THE BLUEPRINT FOR INTERCESSION

Hebrews 7:25 KJV
Wherefore he is able also to save them to the uttermost that come unto God by him, seeing he ever liveth to make intercession for them.

Intercession was an intricate part of every movement and mandate of heaven. From the intercession of the great patriarch Abraham to the apostle Paul, Gods people have engaged in this most vital ministry. The majority of my writings and publications are on the subject of intercession. Interestingly noted in Hebrews 7:25 Christ is identified as an intercessor. Notice that there is a direct correlation to salvation, His eternal mandate and intercession. He is the perfect model and everything about His ministry is worthy of duplication. Apostles, in particular, are mandated to the standards visible in Christ because He sets them in the Church first according to 1 Corinthians 12:28.

The ministry of prayer and the work of intercession is the plumb line that connects the apostle to the power of their sender. Christ stayed connected to His sender, God our Father, through prayer. In eternity He is working because He ever liveth to make intercession. How much more should those He's sending today develop and sustain a culture that's given to the ministry of prayer and the work of intercession.

Luke 3:21 KJV
Now when all the people were baptized, it came to pass, that Jesus also being baptized, and praying, the heaven was opened,

Christ as an apostle was being immersed into His apostolic mandate. To this point in His life He hadn't done much of anything to substantiate His ministry. However this was the turning point and exponential power was about to flow through His ministry. The catalyst for this of course was the fact that He was praying. As a result the heavens opened over Him and all the resources He needed as an apostle were being deployed. Just as Christ needed an open heaven so do those He's sending today. Christ method for opening the heavens was prayer. This model works and should be embraced by those who pattern their ministries after Him.

Luke 6:12-19 KJV
And it came to pass in those days, that he went out into a mountain to pray, and continued all night in prayer to God. 13 And when it was day, he called unto him his disciples: and of them he chose twelve, whom also he named apostles; 14 Simon, (whom he also named

Peter,) and Andrew his brother, James and John, Philip and Bartholomew, 15 Matthew and Thomas, James the son of Alphaeus, and Simon called Zelotes, 16 And Judas the brother of James, and Judas Iscariot, which also was the traitor. 17 And he came down with them, and stood in the plain, and the company of his disciples, and a great multitude of people out of all Judaea and Jerusalem, and from the sea coast of Tyre and Sidon, which came to hear him, and to be healed of their diseases; 18 And they that were vexed with unclean spirits: and they were healed. 19 And the whole multitude sought to touch him: for there went virtue out of him, and healed them all.

And it came to pass in those days really lays the foundation for the referenced verses. The Pharisees were filled with indignation against Christ and were plotting on what they might do to harm Him. Jesus withdraws to a mountain and goes into all night intercession. During that night of prayer power was being deployed by heaven and something of eternal magnitude was about to hit the planet. Jesus would have clarity on choosing His team.

These members were all tied to His destiny, fulfillment of prophecy and the advancement of the Kingdom of God. The stakes couldn't have been higher. In the natural the proponents of darkness were conspiring to inflict bodily harm, but Christ was focused on fulfilling

His commission. This is a noteworthy earmark for apostolic ministry gifts today. Satan will deploy his messengers and they will conspire against you. Withdrawing for times of all night prayer is an apostolic strategy needed to stay focused on the things that concern eternity.

His team is assembled and power is upon Him to influence the multitudes. He stands in the plain with His disciples and multitudes pour out unto Him from all over the land. They came to hear His words, be healed by Him and delivered of their demons. All night prayer is essential to the expanding of the apostle's ministry and them having power to righteously impact the multitudes.

Luke 9:28-29 KJV
And it came to pass about an eight days after these sayings, he took Peter and John and James, and went up into a mountain to pray. 29 And as he prayed, the fashion of his countenance was altered, and his raiment was white and glistering.

Christ ascends to a mountain again and this time He has team members with Him. As He presses into prayer His countenance is changed and the glory of God is manifesting. I believe there are realms of glory we have to labor in prayer in order to access. The glory of God provides a plethora of benefits. Jesus as an apostle prayed until glory came upon Him. 1 Chronicles 7 also has recorded where King Solomon prayed until the glory of God descended in the temple of Solomon. The glory of God is needed in an apostle's ministry. There are certain powers that are aligned with the forces of darkness that would move until God's weighty presence descends on them. The prayers and intercession of the apostles and apostolic believers are vehicles for the Glory of God to manifest. Creating a personal and corporate culture of prayer is an important aspect of an apostle's ministry.

After Jesus descends from this mountain He is met with an extreme case of demonization. His disciples couldn't handle the situation. The Lord reprimands them for their unbelief and then deals with the demon spirit responsible for tormenting the young man brought to His disciples. Christ had accessed a realm of glory and the stronghold of darkness tormenting the child had no choice but to leave. Many of you may say oh, but those cases are reserved for Jesus. However Jesus said He'd work with us and confirm His word with signs following. He shows us how to take our mission to elevated levels of power and that is by praying.

Luke 11:1 KJV
And it came to pass, that, as he was praying in a certain place, when he ceased, one of his disciples said unto

him, Lord, teach us to pray, as John also taught his disciples.

The disciples by now saw such a consistency and discipline in their leaders life, regarding prayer, that they desired to pray. They saw firsthand how Christ flowed effortlessly in the power of God with signs following after coming out of the place of prayer. Once again the one sent derives their authority and power from the one who sends them. Thus Christ engaging His Sender (God Our Father) in prayer was needed for the supply of power required to fulfill His apostolic mission.

Apostles are tasked to teach their followers to duplicate the works they are spearheading as well. Their ministries are literally resources to those whom they are sent. Therefore their disciples must be able to duplicate and effectively model them. If not the move will be one dimensional and limited advancement will occur. Team ministry is vital to the progression of apostolic works, especially the work of prayer and intercession.

Luke 22:40-45 KJV
And when he was at the place, he said unto them, Pray that ye enter not into temptation. 41 And he was withdrawn from them about a stone's cast, and kneeled down, and prayed, 42 Saying, Father, if thou be willing, remove this cup from me: nevertheless not my will, but

thine, be done. 43 And there appeared an angel unto him from heaven, strengthening him. 44 And being in an agony he prayed more earnestly: and his sweat was as it were great drops of blood falling down to the ground. 45 And when he rose up from prayer, and was come to his disciples, he found them sleeping for sorrow,

Christ was at a very pivotal time in His ministry. Humanity was weighing in the balances and the gravity of His coming had suddenly broken forth. Christ models tremendous poise during this taxing time. There were dark forces working to lure Him away from the place of prayer and thus restrict Him from finishing His apostolic assignment. There will be times in the life of every apostle's life where the weight of your mandate and the gravity of your calling collide with your humanity. The thought of giving up along with the pressure tactics of hell could easily become overbearing and break you. Let me encourage you to press into the place of prayer and don't leave until you get Gods approval and glory upon you. Jesus labored in prayer and pressed until all of His human tendencies became subject to God's will. He arose strengthened by God and endured the cross that was awaiting Him.

We all have a cross to bear on a daily basis. There will be times when the journey demands more than you have to give. Just know that the one who sent you has more than enough to sustain you. His pattern for us is to engage Him in prayer until He responds. Persevere until your Sender resources you with the resources of eternity as Christ our apostle.

Today's apostle's who have given themselves to model the works of Christ will be visible and highly involved in the mandate of prayer. They'll be seen leading the charge along with prophets who they serve with in corporate prayer. They will have a personal life that's fueled with passionate prayer as well.

CHAPTER 7

CHRIST THE TEACHER AND DISPENCER OF DOCTRINE

John 3:1-2 KJV
There was a man of the Pharisees, named Nicodemus, a ruler of the Jews: 2 The same came to Jesus by night, and said unto him, Rabbi, we know that thou art a teacher come from God: for no man can do these miracles that thou doest, except God be with him.

Christ as an apostle became one with everything He taught. This is important for apostolic ministry gifts. What we teach and our doctrine should be synonymous with who we are. Christ was the Word made manifest in the flesh. He embodied what He taught. There are some who will seek to teach whatever is trendy or deemed popular in order to gain attention in the realm of men. Apostles versed in multiple subjects will often be found teaching in accordance with their passion.

Notice how Nicodemus sought Christ out. He was ruler in the realm of religion, but deep within he knew he was void of something. He declares, to Christ, we know thou art a teacher come from God. So obviously the teaching ministry was impacting Nicodemus and some of his colleagues, even though as a whole, they sought how they might do Him harm. Nicodemus identifies Christ teaching ministry as a source of miracles. I believe the teaching ministry of an apostle should provide context and content for the flow of miracles.

Some of the breakthroughs the multitudes need and the miracles they are positioned to receive will come as a result of sound teaching and correct doctrine. One of the challenges for the Church throughout the ages has been centered on doctrine. People live by what they are taught. Wrong doctrine, false teaching and theological error are all sources for destructive living and behavior amongst the saints.

I believe that correct doctrine will always encourage and promote healthy growth that will eventually lead to Christ being glorified. Sound doctrine and scriptural integrity within the Church is a burden all apostles share. Churches led by apostles will demonstrate, as a culture, commitment to study and the development of sound doctrine on subject matters they are called to. The fruit of this will be seen in the productivity and sound living of those who ascribe to the teaching. They will be empowered by the principles they glean from and what they've have been taught. The fruit of the teaching will speak for itself.

Mark 6:2 KJV

And when the sabbath day was come, he began to teach in the synagogue: and many hearing him were astonished, saying, From whence hath this man these things? and what wisdom is this which is given unto him, that even such mighty works are wrought by his hands?

The teaching ministry of Christ as an apostle was the catalyst for Him disbursing wisdom and performing mighty works among the multitudes. Faith to obey God and do exploits in His Name is rooted in sound doctrine. When doctrine is lacking unbelief and low level exploits will prevail.

Matthew 7:28-29 KJV

And it came to pass, when Jesus had ended these sayings, the people were astonished at his doctrine:
29 For he taught them as one having authority, and not as the scribes.

Jesus taught as one of authority and His doctrine literally amazed His audiences. His words came with piercing conviction that challenged those who were listening to their very core. His doctrine shifted perspectives and challenged thought paradigms that were reckless and noncompliant. These verses are the response of the audience that heard Jesus addressing the subject of building on a proper foundation. He highlights two kinds of people. The first are those who heard His message and followed through. The second are those who heard and didn't comply. The one who complied and laid a foundation to support what Christ declared would be able to withstand and handle the storm that was to come. The house they would build after the storm settles would remain intact. The one who failed to steward what was taught and cultivate the proper foundation would suffer great loss. The apostolic teaching grace is central to developing believers who can withstand the storms of life. I'm convinced that needless causalities have happened to believers who never have the opportunity to hear truths that challenge our foundations in the word. Apostolic doctrine provokes the hearers to strengthen their foundations.

Luke 5:3 KJV
And he entered into one of the ships, which was Simon's, and prayed him that he would thrust out a little from the land. And he sat down, and taught the people out of the ship.

Jesus came upon a disgruntled fisherman named Simon. The net he was washing when Jesus showed up was his method and the waters he fished were his mission field. Simon also called Peter had toiled all night and came back to the shores empty. His situation was about to change suddenly. He allowed Christ the apostle to begin teaching from his boat. Faith was being built for something supernatural to manifest. He's commanded to launch out. His obedience gave him access to a catch of epic proportion. The teaching ministry of an apostle will address and correct the deficiencies of those who adhere to their doctrine.

Luke 5:17 KJV

And it came to pass on a certain day, as he was teaching, that there were Pharisees and doctors of the law sitting by, which were come out of every town of Galilee, and Judaea, and Jerusalem: and the power of the Lord was present to heal them.

The teaching ministry of Christ the apostle was a conduit for healing to flow. God's word is like a medicine. He sends it to heal and deliver His people. God Himself is the Word and He is also a Healer. The assimilation of His word as doctrine is designed to address the ills in the lives of those who come into contact with the Word. Remember that part of the mandate of an apostle is to represent the one who sends them.

Apostles today who have patterned their ministries after Christ apostolic model will have formidable teaching ministries. They will major on doctrine, but also the Spirit as well. They will demonstrate what they teach and model it before the masses. They will at times labor on subject matters for long periods of time. This is necessary to get people established in the faith and develop them to manifest what they have been taught.

Christ as an apostle had 6 primary teachings that made up His doctrine. They are evident in the Gospels, The Acts of the Apostles and The Epistles of Paul. Hebrews 6 lists them as repentance from dead works, faith towards God, baptisms, laying on of hands, resurrection from the dead and eternal judgment. Within the mandate of apostles you will at one point or another hear them expound on these principle teachings.

CHAPTER 8

THE PREACHING MINSTRY OF CHRIST

Luke 4:18-19 KJV
The Spirit of the Lord is upon me, because he hath anointed me to preach the gospel to the poor; he hath sent me to heal the brokenhearted, to preach deliverance to the captives, and recovering of sight to the blind, to set at liberty them that are bruised, 19 To preach the acceptable year of the Lord.

Jesus is quoting from the prophet Isaiah and emphasizing 6 types of anointing that were upon Him or 6 things He was anointed to do. Christ proclaims three of them were to preach.

1) To **Preach** The Gospel To The Poor

2) To Heal The Broken Hearted

3) To **Preach** Deliverance To The Captive

4) To Recover The Sight of The Blind

5) To Set At Liberty Them That Are Bruised

6) To **Preach** The Acceptable Year of The Lord

I'm convinced that preaching is an apostolic function according to the words of Christ, the perfect apostle. The word preach(ed, ing) occurs over 130 times alone in the New Testament alone. One of its primary meanings is to herald as a public crier, especially of divine truth. The preaching ministry of Christ and apostles patterned after Him is vital for proclaiming the Good News, The Gospel.

Jesus preached the Gospel and heralds an announcement of the coming of The Kingdom of God. The heralding dimension of apostolic preaching helps to prepare the hearts of people for that, which is certain to come. God anoints their preaching in order to destroy the yokes and burdens upon the recipients of their messages restricted to an old paradigm or subdued by an old wine skin.

Jesus preached repentance to the masses. The word repent means to change the way you think. Those who hear The Gospel and do not change their thinking can't reap of the benefits brought by the message or the messenger. I believe it takes anointed preaching to liberate the masses. People who are broken, in a state of disarray, delusional, hurting, overwhelmed with cares, under heavy yokes and on the brink of total breakdown need the anointing. It worked for those who were inundated with darkness and despair during Christ earthly ministry and it will today. He modeled an eternal pattern that's worthy of being duplicated. God has chosen the foolishness of preaching to save them that believe according to 1 Corinthians 1:21.

Apostles will also move in what is known as polemic preaching. Their message will come with strong conviction and often stir the indignation of the Lord. People will be activated for war and hostile confrontation. This will not be aimed towards flesh and blood, but rather against the powers of darkness.

Polemic preaching causes demons to manifest and often serves as a conduit for miracles to flow. Polemic preaching provokes Gods justice and judgment. False doctrine and the works of hell that hold people captive through lies and deceit are also targets of polemic preaching. Apostles are graced for polemic preaching and are set to defend the truth by confronting erroneous and heretical assignments against the Church or the territories they're sent to liberate.

What Are Some Benefits of Apostolic Preaching?

Preaching is a catalyst for the demonstration of glad tidings of the Kingdom of God. People are compelled to do great works. Luke 8:1-3 KJV

Preaching provokes the supernatural. Jesus, after preaching, would often move into a time of miracles, deliverance of the bound and healing of the sick. Matthew 9:35KJV

Preaching can be a type of battering ram as with Phillip when he breaks into Samaria. An entire city gave heed to the things he declared concerning the Kingdom of God. He also demonstrates the Kingdom by healing the sick and flowing in miracles. Acts 8:12 KJV

Preaching provides power to establish people in the faith. There is also an unveiling of mysteries activated through apostolic preaching. Romans 16:25 KJV

Preaching is a vehicle for the manifestation or appearance of Gods word. It's through preaching that many will see tangible miracles. Preaching serves as a means of infiltrating the kingdoms of this world and supernaturally influencing those within them. Matthew 10:1 displays the Word in their lives.

Preaching releases the Power of God for salvation. Romans 1:15-16

Preaching looses a summons for the Lord to stand with and strengthen His people. 2 Timothy 4:17

Preaching provokes a demonstration of the Spirit and power. 1 Corinthians 2:4

CHAPTER 9

CHRIST THE ULTIMATE TEAM BUILDER

Team ministry is essential for the advancement of any organization or corporation. The networking of multiple parts helps to service the overall vested interest of the organization or corporation. When it comes to the advancement of the Kingdom of God, team ministry is extremely important. From the beginning God was displaying team ministry in the context of creation. Genesis 1 reveals 8 times where God said "let us." His counsel or Godhead was involved in the creation process and thus we see team ministry in action. After God creates man He determines it's not good for him to be alone and then He creates a helper for man. This team would be identified as marriage and God Himself would establish a basis of fellowship.

Matthew 10:1 KJV
And when he had called unto him his twelve disciples, he gave them power against unclean spirits, to cast them out, and to heal all manner of sickness and all manner of disease.

Mark 6:7 KJV
And he called unto him the twelve, and began to send them forth by two and two; and gave them power over unclean spirits;

Luke 9:1 KJV
Then he called his twelve disciples together, and gave them power and authority over all devils, and to cure diseases.

Jesus was very intentional about building His team. His aim was to develop able ministry gifts that could flow within His model and extend the rule of His Kingdom. Christ authorized and empowered them to impact people on the same level and with the same magnitude as He did. He invested 3 years of night and day impartation with a group of teenagers. They caught His mantle, received of His spirit and pushed His mandate to the ends of the earth.

Synergy is a very important aspect of team ministry because it mandates that every part does its part for the greater good. Apostolic teams bring synergy to the Church as a whole. They help mobilize and activate local assemblies to move beyond restrictions imposed upon them by the territorial powers bent on limiting the Kingdom.

Jesus understood that if His Kingdom was to have continuity after His ascension, He needed teams in place. Apostles today must understand the magnitude of their apostleship that mandates the development and deployment of teams. Jesus not only raised up the 12 but He also commissioned 70 as well.

Luke 10:1-2 KJV

After these things the Lord appointed other seventy also, and sent them two and two before his face into every city and place, whither he himself would come. 2 Therefore said he unto them, The harvest truly is great, but the labourers are few: pray ye therefore the Lord of the harvest, that he would send forth labourers into his harvest.

The 70 were sent in teams of two into cities that Christ would visit. Teams are needed to break regions open and establish them in present truth or activate gifts and graces needed to advance. Jesus declares that the harvest is great but the labourers are few. Apostolic ministry is one of labour. The forming and deployment of teams helps to ease the labor. Apostles will build teams with capacity to minister in the areas of deliverance, prophecy, worship, intercession, evangelism, miracles, healing, spiritual warfare and those who can impart sound doctrine. They will release grace and wisdom to influence the harvest.

Jesus still desires to touch cities and territories today. Apostles must give themselves to training ministry gifts in the local church and the nations and imparting their burden for the globe. Resources will be allocated to send teams and influence distant lands. They will help build passion and excitement within their local church and ministry affiliations for the disenfranchised, the persecuted church, dark places in the earth and grids controlled by proponents of darkness.

The commissioning of an apostle requires they build a team. A seal of their apostleship will be emphasized by the team(s) they build. The task and charge heavens puts on them is far greater than their anointing alone. They are graced to share the burden God places on them. Prophets will be drawn to apostles. Apostles and prophets make formidable teams.

The apostolic team is created by the apostle who looks for skillful builders in the course of their travels. It is formed on his initiatives though ultimately it is the Holy Spirit who links the team together. (Jonathan David)

Apostles have the capacity and wisdom to gather skillful ministry gifts and also develop them if they are set over a local church. God sends them by His wisdom and the wisdom of God will be a visible earmark of their ministry. Apostles are called wise master builders and they understand what and who is needed to complete the task at hand, because the blueprint is understood. They will gather and build teams suitable for the work at hand.

Biblical Teams & Apostolic Types

Numbers 11:25 KJV

And the Lord came down in a cloud, and spake unto him, and took of the spirit that was upon him, and gave it unto the seventy elders: and it came to pass, that, when the spirit rested upon them, they prophesied, and did not cease.

Moses had an apostolic type team. In Exodus 24 he is commanded by God to come before Him and worship. This is the forming of a team. Moses was sent by God and needed a team to fulfill his commission. Impartation comes upon the 70 and the spirit that rested on Moses came on them.

Apostles understand the importance of impartation in order for their team to function efficiently. The team assembled by Moses began to prophesy and did not cease. Moses was able to align himself with the vision ordained by God and still minister to the needs of the people because of his team.

Numbers 13:1-3 KJV

And the Lord spake unto Moses, saying, 2 Send thou men, that they may search the land of Canaan, which I give unto the children of Israel: of every tribe of their fathers shall ye send a man, everyone a ruler among them. 3 And Moses by the commandment of the Lord sent them from the wilderness of Paran: all those men were heads of the children of Israel.

Moses was tasked with the recruiting 12 rulers from the 12 tribes and sending them to spy out the land that God was giving Israel as an inheritance. They were to bring back a report consistent with what God had declared. In their quest to advance and further the Kingdom of God apostles will at times gather leaders and deploy them into distant lands and dark places. The aim will be to plant works or connect with churches in that territory and strengthen them. There is a need for these apostles, of this measure, to have prophets on their team who can both discern and identify those with the grace and capacity necessary for the task.

Only two out of those sent by Moses brought a righteous report. One of the challenges when expansion and pioneering exploits come upon apostolic teams is to make sure you build with people who can think big and have a frontiersmen spirit. They must have a passion for new things and exploits. Caleb who was a ruler in Judah and Joshua were the two. They had a formidable spirit and largeness of heart, two necessary attributes to be joined to an apostolic team. May your Caleb's and Joshua's come forth.

Acts 11:25-26 KJV
Then departed Barnabas to Tarsus, for to seek Saul:

26 And when he had found him, he brought him unto Antioch. And it came to pass, that a whole year they assembled themselves with the church, and taught much people. And the disciples were called Christians first in Antioch.

The Church was in a time of transition and persecution. They were experiencing a scattering, but the hand of God was mighty upon them and the Kingdom was expanding rapidly. Barnabas joins forces with Saul who is also called Paul. They targeted Antioch and launched a Kingdom campaign that lasted one year. This apostolic team impacted multitudes and kingdom disciples began to emerge in that region. Apostolic teams are needed for disciple making. The Kingdom of God has greater thrust in regions where disciples are developed.

Acts 15:22, 27 & 32 KJV

Then pleased it the apostles and elders, with the whole church, to send chosen men of their own company to Antioch with Paul and Barnabas; namely, Judas surnamed Barabbas and Silas, chief men among the brethren: 27 We have sent therefore Judas and Silas, who shall also tell you the same things by mouth. 32 And Judas and Silas, being prophets also themselves, exhorted the brethren with many words, and confirmed them.

Judas and Silas are prophets, but they form an apostolic team. A core of apostolic leaders sent them and their ministry brought much encouragement to Antioch. Apostles recognize the need for prophets and will place tremendous value upon them. Prophets help the Church on so many levels. One major area is helping the Church stay aligned with Christ according to Ephesians 2:20. Judas and Silas were prophets of utterance.

They exhorted the brethren with many words, which literally means to call them near. They had at their disposal a supernatural draw activated by their utterances. Apostolic teams, comprised of prophets, will challenge the Church to come to higher levels concerning the Spirit. Their words will be the catalyst for this to happen.

Acts 15:39-41 KJV
And the contention was so sharp between them, that they departed asunder one from the other: and so Barnabas took Mark, and sailed unto Cyprus; 40 And Paul chose Silas, and departed, being recommended by the brethren unto the grace of God. 41 And he went through Syria and Cilicia, confirming the churches.

Challenges will arise when wrong personalities are paired or when pride gets in the equation. Humility is one of the most potent aspects of an apostolic team. Those who lack in the area of humility will make for a terrible team member. Apostolic teams must be humble and embrace preferring one another. After the separation of Barnabas and Paul a new team emerges between Paul and Silas. This team does a phenomenal job in breaking into new territories. They influenced many churches and initiated new plants as well. The team they forged was graced to confirm churches which means to support, further, reestablish and strengthen. There are some churches that need to be reestablished in order for the strength they need to manifest. Apostolic teams are deployed to support churches and reestablish them in present truth. They can upgrade those houses in areas where strength may be lacking and impart truths that might not be know.

Attributes of Apostolic Teams

Loyalty - is fidelity and capacity to remain truthful to relationships, assignments, obligations and duties necessary for Kingdom Advancement.

Faithfulness - to remain consistent at all times regardless of situations or circumstances. The aim is the Kingdom and the furtherance of the Gospel.

Transparency – will be present in order to model vulnerability to the point of exposure of ones frailties without fear of criticism or fear of acceptance.

Stewardship – as it relates the ability to manage another's goods in the way they themselves would.

Honor - so that appreciation and value can flourish for those whom God has gifted and graced to works beyond that of ones self.

Integrity –is necessary for moral soundness required for upholding and adhering righteous standards.

Discipleship– is required in order to abide teachable and consistently willing to follow Kingdom principles that will foster both personal and corporate growth.

Humility - so genuine value in Christ is established for those on your team so you can purposefully esteem them.

Meekness –for the ability to embrace the role of being virtuous when vices are present that oppose you.

Honesty - the capacity to be forthright regardless of the cost and be truthful at all times.

Accountability - to consistently give account for your gifts, talents and time by balancing your life out to reconcile with the vision of the set man.

Trustworthiness - so that a personal culture is established in order to assure your team members, you will be and do what is required for the team.

There are other formidable teams through the scriptures that are noteworthy. My prayer is that as you continue to pursue Christ as your apostle and ministry model for the ages that a supply will manifest and thoroughly furnish all of your endeavors to advance His Kingdom. May the grace and peace of the Almighty prevail as you grow in the knowledge of Christ.

MORE GREAT RESOURCES FROM
STEPHEN A. GARNER MINISTRIES

Books

- 50 Lessons Ministry Has Taught Me
- Apostolic Pioneering
- Benefits of Praying in Tongues
- Essentials of the Prophetic, Revised and Expanded
- Exposing the Spirit of Anger
- Fundamentals of Deliverance 101, Revised and Expanded
- Kingdom Prayer
- Ministering Spirits: "Engaging the Angelic Realm"
- Overcoming Satanic Entanglements
- Pray Without Ceasing, Special Edition
- Restoring Prophetic Watchmen
- Deliver Us From Evil
- The Blessing
- The Kingdom of God: A Believer's Guide to Kingdom Living
- Prayers, Decrees & Confessions for Wisdom
- Prayers, Decrees & Confessions for Favour & Grace
- Prayers, Decrees & Confessions for Prosperity
- Prayers, Decrees & Confessions for Increase
- Prayers, Decrees & Confessions for Righteousness, Revised & Expanded
- Prayers, Decrees & Confessions for Goodness & Mercy
- Prayers, Decrees & Confessions for Power
- Prayers, Decrees & Confessions for Rewards
- Prayers that Strengthen Marriages and Families

CD's

- Prayers For The Nations
- Prayers Against Python & Witchcraft
- Prayers Of Healing & Restoration
- Prayers of Renunciation and Deliverance
- Thy Kingdom Come
- The Glory
- Overcoming Spirits of Terrorism
- Recompense Of Rewards
- The Spirit of the Breaker
- The Fear of the Lord

CONTACT INFORMATION

STEPHEN A. GARNER MINISTRIES
P.O. BOX 1545, BOLINGBROOK, IL 60440
EMAIL: SAGARNERMINISTRIES@GMAIL.COM
WWW.SAGMINISTRIES.COM

CPSIA information can be obtained
at www.ICGtesting.com
Printed in the USA
LVHW08s1333260918
591433LV00016B/362/P

9 781719 339278